MECHANICAL ENGINEERING
IN THE REAL WORLD

by M. M. Eboch

Content Consultant
Ebrahim Asadi
Assistant Professor of Mechanical Engineering
University of Memphis

Core Library

An Imprint of Abdo Publishing
abdopublishing.com

abdopublishing.com

Published by Abdo Publishing, a division of ABDO, PO Box 398166, Minneapolis, Minnesota 55439. Copyright © 2017 by Abdo Consulting Group, Inc. International copyrights reserved in all countries. No part of this book may be reproduced in any form without written permission from the publisher. Core Library™ is a trademark and logo of Abdo Publishing.

Printed in the United States of America, North Mankato, Minnesota
082016
012017

THIS BOOK CONTAINS
RECYCLED MATERIALS

Cover Photo: Lai Xinlin/Imaginechina/AP Images
Interior Photos: Lai Xinlin/Imaginechina/AP Images, 1; Richard Marshall/The St. Paul Pioneer Press/AP Images, 4, 43; iStockphoto, 7, 22 (top left), 22 (top right); Reed Saxon/AP Images, 11; Keren Su/Getty Images, 14; Claudio Divizia/Hemera/Thinkstock, 17; SPL/Science Source, 19; Steven van Soldt/iStockphoto, 22 (bottom left); John Gollop/iStockphoto, 22 (bottom right); Brian Bell/Science Source, 24; Jason Clark/The Evansville Courier & Press/AP Images, 29, 45; David Royal/Monterey County Herald/AP Images, 31; Patrick Pleul/Picture-Alliance/DPA/AP Images, 32; Ann Hermes/The Christian Science Monitor/AP Images, 34; Geoff Brightling/DK Images, 37; Disability Images/Science Source, 39

Editor: Arnold Ringstad
Series Designer: Ryan Gale

Publisher's Cataloging-in-Publication Data

Names: Eboch, M. M., author.
Title: Mechanical engineering in the real world / by M. M. Eboch.
Description: Minneapolis, MN : Abdo Publishing, 2017. | Series: STEM in the real
    world | Includes bibliographical references and index.
Identifiers: LCCN 2016945472 | ISBN 9781680784817 (lib. bdg.) |
    ISBN 9781680798661 (ebook)
Subjects: LCSH: Mechanical engineering--Juvenile literature.
Classification: DDC 621--dc23
LC record available at http://lccn.loc.gov/2016945472

CONTENTS

CHAPTER ONE
What Is Mechanical Engineering?   4

CHAPTER TWO
Mechanical Engineering History   14

CHAPTER THREE
Careers in Mechanical Engineering   24

CHAPTER FOUR
The Future of Mechanical Engineering   34

Fast Facts 42

Stop and Think 44

Glossary 46

Learn More 47

Index 48

About the Author 48

WHAT IS MECHANICAL ENGINEERING?

A strange car drives down the street. It is small, with only two seats. The dark gray sides look rough. The top is open to the air. This is the Strati. It is the first of its kind. This car was made on a three-dimensional (3D) printer.

The Strati belongs to Jay Rogers. He runs a company called Local Motors. Rogers thought too much money was wasted in designing cars. He had a

Engineers can now use 3D printers to build cars, whether small models or full-size versions.

new idea. The body of this car is made from a strong plastic. A 3D printer built up each part of it in layers. In approximately 40 hours, the 3D printer made a car. Some parts, such as the motor, were made separately. Still, most of the car was made on the printer.

This is a new way of thinking about making cars. Most cars are made on factory assembly lines. Machines and workers make thousands of the same parts. Then they combine these parts into identical cars. With 3D printing, cars are made one at a time. A customer could design his or her own car. The finished product might look different from any other car. As the process gets better, printing cars will be faster and cheaper. The technology could be used to make many cars at a low cost. These cars could even be recycled. Each one can be melted down. Then that plastic can be used to print a new car. Manufacturing objects, whether by traditional factories or 3D printers, is one of the main jobs of mechanical engineers.

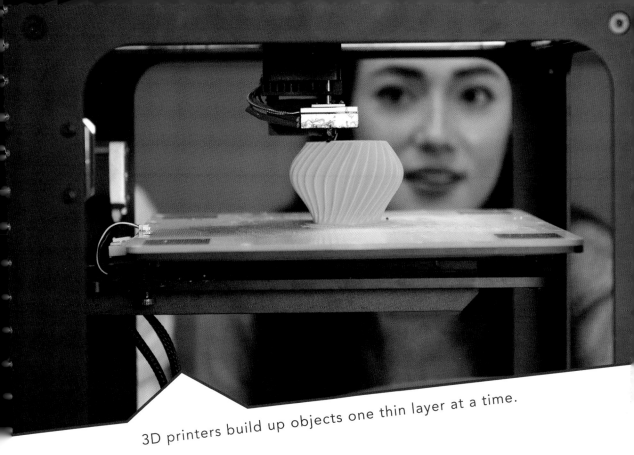

3D printers build up objects one thin layer at a time.

Mechanical Engineers at Work

The 3D printer is a great example of engineering at work. Engineers use science to solve problems. They design and build things to make life easier.

Engineers work in different areas. Mechanical engineers design and build machines of all types. Some design the engines in cars, boats, trains, and planes. Others may work with machinery at power plants or factories. Mechanical engineers also develop smaller items. They build medical devices and computers. They even invent new toys.

Many Branches

Engineering has several branches. They include civil, chemical, electrical, and mechanical engineering. Mechanical engineering is the largest branch. It includes many specialties. Vehicle engineers design vehicles such as cars and ships. Aerospace engineers design aircraft and spacecraft. Acoustical engineers work with sound and vibration. Thermal engineers study how heat transfers between things. They design heating and cooling equipment. Manufacturing engineers design and make products. These fields are all part of mechanical engineering.

The objects made by mechanical engineers are found around the world. They are even found in space. Space travel depends on good mechanical engineering. In 2012 NASA sent the *Curiosity* rover to Mars. By 2016 the robot was still driving on the planet's surface. More than 7,000 people worked on *Curiosity*. Many of them were mechanical engineers. They designed and built it. They tested its parts to make sure things worked. They successfully sent the rover through space to another planet. The skills of the mission's mechanical engineers helped make the rover a success.

A New Tool for Engineers

3D printers are one of the many tools used by today's engineers. They use 3D printers to build things and test new designs. The 3D printer itself was created by an engineer more than 30 years ago.

A person can use a computer program to

IN THE REAL WORLD

Working at NASA

Many astronauts are also mechanical engineers. In the early days of the US space program, most astronauts started in the military. Over time, that changed. Franklin Chang-Diaz studied mechanical engineering and physics. He became an astronaut in 1980. He had not been in the military. Yet Chang-Diaz flew seven missions. In one, he worked on the International Space Station. He made three space walks during that mission. After he left NASA, he set up his own company. He designed technology for space travel. Today it is more common for scientists and engineers to become astronauts without doing military service first.

make a 3D model. Or a 3D scanner can scan an object and convert it to a 3D model. Then the 3D printer takes over. The printer lays down plastic or metal one layer at a time. Soon a three-dimensional object is built.

People have found many uses for 3D printers. They can make bicycles and toys. They are used to design car parts and airplane wings. 3D printing is great for making one-of-a-kind things. The technology is also improving. Someday 3D printers may replace large factories. The 3D printer shows how mechanical engineering is using modern technology. It also shows how mechanical engineering is changing the world.

Idea to Product

Mechanical engineers turn ideas into brand-new objects. They may also make current products better. For example, mechanical engineers have built surgical robots. These robots perform surgery previously done by humans. Now engineers are improving those robots. This will make the robot surgeons safer and

Some mechanical engineers build robots to explore space.

better. They may also be able to perform new types of surgery.

Engineers are also working on flexible display screens. These screens for TVs or computers can be rolled up. A person could roll up his or her TV and store it in a cupboard. A tiny screen could be rolled up and kept in a pen. But this technology is not perfect.

The screens sometimes break as they bend. This leads to blank spots on the display. Engineers will need to solve this problem to make the technology useful. They need a lot of creative thinking to solve problems such as these.

Technology is everywhere in our lives. Mechanical engineers design that technology and keep it working. Their field is critical to our modern world. Mechanical engineers work in many fields, including medicine, military defense, manufacturing, and more. This provides many options for young people who like science. Mechanical engineering is an exciting area of study for today's students.

Dr. Anita Sengupta is an aerospace engineer. She helped design the parachute for NASA's *Curiosity* rover. She now leads a team working on a project for the International Space Station. When asked what she likes about her job, Sengupta said:

> I wanted to do the parachute job because [it was] difficult. I specifically like to take on challenging problems because I like to be pushed beyond my comfort level. I am also an experimentalist and parachutes require a lot of testing to make sure they work. . . . [I]t fit in perfectly with my technical and research background. There were many unknowns in this parachute development because of the size and deployment conditions. . . . I live for the challenge, so it is not stress. It is excitement and satisfaction of accomplishing something of this magnitude.

Source: "Women Talk: 10+ Questions with Rocket Scientist, Dr. Anita Sengupta." Women You Should Know. Outhouse PR, August 27, 2012. Web. Accessed April 13, 2016.

Back It Up

Sengupta is discussing why she enjoys her career, and especially the parachute project. Write a few sentences discussing the point she is making. Then write down a few pieces of evidence she provides to support her point.

MECHANICAL ENGINEERING HISTORY

Engineering has been used for thousands of years. People from around the world helped develop its different branches. Zhang Heng was a Chinese man of many talents. He lived from 78 to 139 CE. He invented a machine to study the stars. It was powered by water. He also invented a device that could detect earthquakes from far away.

Ancient Chinese engineer Zhang Heng created a machine to detect earthquakes.

Al-Jazari was an important Arab inventor. He lived around the year 1200. He invented the first clock that could tell time in minutes. He wrote an engineering book that told how to make many machines. He used water to keep the machine parts moving.

The Age of Engineering in Europe

Leonardo da Vinci was an artist and an engineer. He lived in the 1500s in what is now Italy. He had many creative ideas. He kept notebooks of ideas for new machines. He had several ideas for flying machines. One was an early version of a helicopter. He also designed war machines. One gun with several barrels was similar to a modern machine gun. Centuries before the first automobile, Leonardo designed a cart propelled by springs. It had brakes and a way to steer. Most of these machines were never built. Leonardo did not have the materials and knowledge to make them work.

Some of Leonardo's ideas could work only after new materials were invented. His version of the

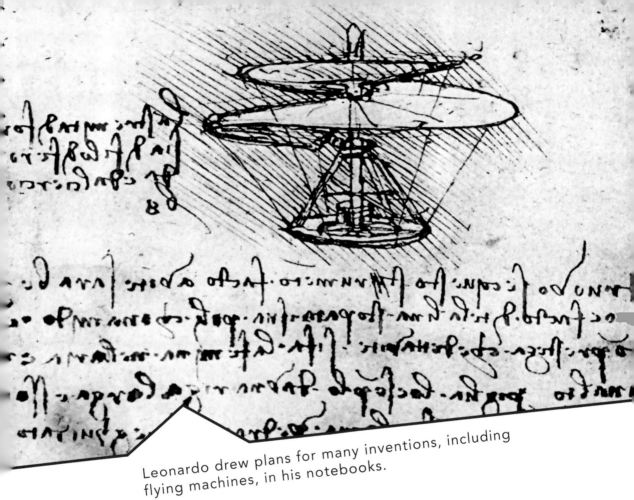

Leonardo drew plans for many inventions, including flying machines, in his notebooks.

helicopter had blades made out of linen. This cloth is not as strong as today's metal blades. He also did not have a good motor. He planned for four men to stand on a central platform turning cranks. This would not have created enough power to allow the invention to fly. In other cases, Leonardo's ideas could never have worked practically. Another flying machine likely would have worked as a glider. But it did not have a way to take off or land safely. Still, Leonardo helped combine art and engineering. Coming up with new ideas is important to engineering.

Modern Engineering

People continued to invent new machines. They also developed new materials. They improved many materials, including metal and concrete. Each advance helped bring about further advances.

Engineers developed new ways to power industries and vehicles. They invented steam engines in the 1700s. This helped launch the Industrial Revolution.

More Math Needed

Math is important to engineering. The central ideas behind math developed over time. People in the Middle East were the first to develop algebra, in the 800s. Algebra includes the concept of an unknown number, called a variable. The ideas of algebra were later refined in Europe. Calculus was developed after that. This branch of mathematics was established in the 1600s. Two men, Isaac Newton and Gottfried Leibniz, came up with calculus separately. Calculus is the study of changes and curves.

Engineers tested steam-powered trains in the United Kingdom in 1829.

Before that, most people made things such as clothes at home. With new steam-powered machines, factories could make clothes faster and more cheaply. Many people moved from farms to cities to work in factories. Steam-powered trains replaced wagons pulled by horses. Steamboats replaced sailboats. These faster trains and ships could move goods quickly across the country or around the world. Engineering was changing life in many ways.

An understanding of electricity led to more new machines. Electric motors and batteries largely replaced steam power after the 1920s. Electrical engineering split from mechanical engineering. It became its own field of study. The internal combustion engine was another big advance. Many inventors experimented with these engines in the 1800s. They entered more general use in the 1900s. These engines are powered by fossil fuels. They are used in cars and many other machines.

By the mid-1900s, the invention of computers changed engineering again. Today mechanical engineers use many computer programs. Computer-aided design (CAD) programs are especially important. They let an engineer design a new object on a computer. Today, advanced 3D printers make it possible for engineers to print those designs as real-life objects.

Schools and Organizations

Early mechanical engineers learned their field on the job or by trial and error. In the early 1800s, European engineers started several schools for formal engineering training. The United States had three schools of engineering by 1825. Around this time, the science of engineering became better understood. Engineering separated into different branches. Mechanical engineering focused on machines.

IN THE REAL WORLD

Automotive Engineering

Mechanical engineers who work in the auto industry help design better vehicles. This could mean cars that are faster, safer, cheaper, or better looking. It could also mean vehicles that do not pollute as much. Some engineers design race cars. A few engineers even drive the race cars. NASCAR driver Ryan Newman has an engineering degree. He won the 2008 Daytona 500. Other engineers work on different vehicles, such as motorcycles. One of the founders of the Harley-Davidson Motor Company studied mechanical engineering.

What Is a Machine?

Mechanical engineers work on all types of machines. Machines have moving parts and use power to do work. This image shows some examples. What kinds of moving parts would you find in these objects? What other examples of powered machines with moving parts can you think of from your daily life?

Today engineering has many branches. These branches often overlap. Engineers must know about fields related to their own. Engineers of different types work together. They also work alongside architects, designers, and scientists.

Mechanical engineers brought about major advances in many fields. They helped invent cars, trains, and airplanes. They designed the machines and factories that are still used to produce modern goods. They helped design movie cameras, radios, and televisions. They even played important roles in the invention of computers and smartphones. Over the last few hundred years, mechanical engineers have changed the world.

EXPLORE ONLINE

Chapter Two discusses some inventions created by mechanical engineers. Go to the website listed below and read about mechanical engineering science fair projects. What new information did you learn about the kinds of things mechanical engineers build?

Mechanical Engineering Science Fair Projects
mycorelibrary.com/mechanical-engineering

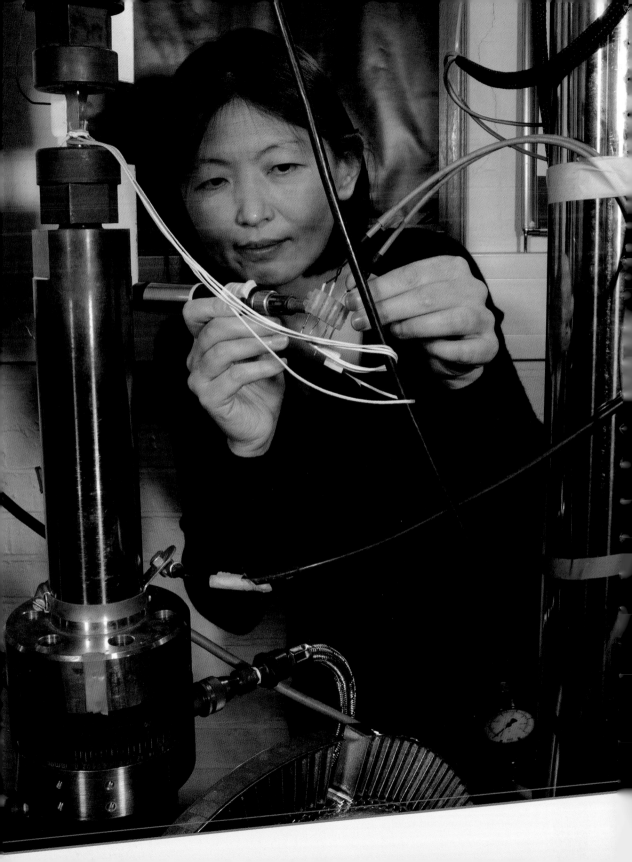

CAREERS IN MECHANICAL ENGINEERING

All mechanical engineers design or build machines. Within the field, there are many different career options. Some mechanical engineers work in product design. They develop or improve products of all types. They may deal with medical devices, gaming systems, robots, or spacecraft.

Mechanical engineers often test individual parts before putting them together into a larger final product.

Other mechanical engineers work in manufacturing. They choose the best materials to build a product, and they design the machines that will make that product. Research and development is another area. Mechanical engineers in this field create ideas for new products. They may develop new materials and techniques. Other engineers use these innovations to produce new products.

Getting Ready

Mechanical engineering is a great field for those who enjoy taking things apart to figure out how they work. A good mechanical engineer also likes solving problems. These engineers tackle many of the problems facing our world. That makes mechanical engineering a great career for those who want to help people.

Students interested in mechanical engineering should take math classes in high school. Programming classes are good too. Much of modern engineering is done on computers.

Often mechanical engineers work in groups. It helps to enjoy working with other people. Engineers also need to explain themselves clearly. They need to write and speak well. Taking a foreign language is a good idea. Many companies that hire mechanical engineers have offices in other countries. Knowing a second language lets a person collaborate with engineers from another country.

Finally, curiosity and creativity are important qualities for any mechanical engineer. Following many interests can give a future engineer a broad range of experiences. Sports, art, and music are all

Safety First

A good mechanical engineer must be able to make important decisions. Mechanical engineers have to decide every detail about a product. They perform tests and calculations. People's lives may depend on this work. For example, mechanical engineers design safety features on cars. A bad design could cause people to get hurt. Fortunately, most engineers work in teams. They can get advice from several people to make sure they make the best decision.

good areas to explore. These activities can also help a person learn to work well with others.

College Success

Mechanical engineers need at least a bachelor's degree in engineering. In college, students will take advanced math classes. They will study chemistry and physics. Special classes cover topics such as robotics, spacecraft design, and nanotechnology. Students also experience hands-on activities in different laboratories.

An internship can help prepare a student for a future career. He or she can get real-world training by working alongside engineers at a company. Internships are also a chance to see what parts of the field a person likes or dislikes.

Many people take their engineering education further. They earn graduate degrees in the field. A master's degree can open up even more job possibilities. A doctorate can prepare a person to do advanced research at a university or at research and

Mechanical engineering students at several universities develop and test extremely efficient solar-powered cars.

development sections of companies. Researchers make exciting new discoveries at the cutting edge of mechanical engineering.

On the Job

The US Department of Labor tracks wages for jobs in different fields. As of 2015, the typical yearly salary for a mechanical engineer was more than $83,000. A background in mechanical engineering can be useful in other fields as well. Engineers get training in problem solving and creative thinking. They tend to have good attention to detail. These qualities help them do well in many fields. Some people with engineering degrees go on to careers in medicine, law, banking, or finance. Some teach engineering classes. Engineers working at colleges and universities often have other duties besides teaching. They manage labs and oversee research.

Because mechanical engineers do many different jobs, the kinds of work they do can look very different. Some engineers work in offices or labs. Others work

IN THE REAL WORLD

Teaching the Next Group

Bill Nye studied mechanical engineering. Then he worked for a company that makes airplanes. He worked as an engineer during the day. At night, he did standup comedy. Later he became a full-time comedy writer and performer. He hosted a television show that taught kids about science. It was called *Bill Nye the Science Guy*. The show ran for 100 episodes.

A US Navy mechanical engineer demonstrates a new engineering project to US secretary of the navy Ray Mabus.

outside at construction sites. Engineers may work for the government, the military, or a private company. They can become consultants, providing expert engineering advice to businesses around the world.

Some mechanical engineers travel to meet clients. They may set up equipment in the field. For example, a mechanical engineer working on wind power could

Mechanical engineers who deal with wind turbines may have to work at great heights.

help install machines on wind farms around the country. Some engineering companies have branches in multiple countries. This means engineers may even have the chance to work in another country. A mechanical engineering degree gives a person a wide variety of career choices.

FURTHER EVIDENCE

Chapter Three introduced you to some jobs in mechanical engineering. What was the main point of this chapter? What evidence is included to support this point? Go to the website below. Explore some of the other employment opportunities for mechanical engineers. Does the information support the chapter's main points?

Science Buddies: Mechanical Engineer
mycorelibrary.com/mechanical-engineering

CHAPTER FOUR

THE FUTURE OF MECHANICAL ENGINEERING

The future has many challenges for engineers around the world. More than 7 billion people live on our planet. They all need food and clean water. They need energy. Providing these things safely and cheaply is not easy. Engineering solutions could give many people better lives.

Mechanical engineering is bringing many new tools to medicine. Biomedical engineering is a

Engineers around the world are developing energy-efficient technologies, including improved lighting systems.

Making New Body Parts

3D printers can make new body parts. People today are using hands and legs made on 3D printers. Each one can be custom-made for that person. Several people have had parts of their skulls replaced with 3D printed pieces. In the future, 3D printers will make even more body parts. Soon 3D printers will be making hearts and other organs. The printers will make skin for burn victims. The army plans to help wounded soldiers this way. The printers are also used to make medical equipment. Small hospitals can print items they need right away.

growing area. This field uses engineering to solve problems in health care. Engineers design artificial body parts to replace real ones that are missing or injured. Artificial arms and legs with complex moving parts help people live more ordinary lives. Some of these limbs can even be controlled by the patient's brain. Tomorrow's engineers will likely improve this technology and invent new solutions to medical problems.

Nanotechnology is another growing field. It involves the engineering

Nanotechnology

One day we may use machines too small for humans to see. They may even move through the bloodstream to repair the body. The above illustration shows one artist's vision of what such a machine might look like. What kinds of other things could such small machines do? How might they differ from larger machines? Would their small size introduce new dangers?

of systems on a very small scale. Imagine a robot or computer so small you need a microscope to see it. This technology has many uses. It could improve medicine. It may change the way we make products.

The military will also find uses for this technology. It may become widespread in the coming decades.

Meeting Challenges

Environmentally friendly technology is an important and growing field. This type of technology tries to meet society's needs while creating as little pollution as possible. Many products can help do this. Batteries can be recharged instead of thrown away. Electricity can power cars without the pollution created by fossil fuels. New energy

Alternative energy sources, including solar panels, are a major area of work for today's mechanical engineers.

sources might generate electrical power for homes and businesses with less pollution.

Mechanical engineers are developing new devices and systems to harness these forms of alternative energy. They are designing turbines to capture the energy from the wind. They are creating devices to turn the energy of a rushing river into electrical power.

They are also finding ways to reduce the pollution created by our existing energy sources.

Scientists and engineers are making improvements in all these areas. Yet much more work needs to be done. These machines need to work well and be reliable. They need to be safe for people and the environment. Mechanical engineers will create a cleaner future for the world.

Doug Lucht is a mechanical engineer. He works on heating, ventilating, and air conditioning (HVAC) systems. He describes how modern technology is changing the way people in his career think about energy:

> As an HVAC engineer, we have a unique opportunity to help save energy consumption for new and existing buildings. A large percentage of the energy that is used in the United States goes to heating and cooling buildings. . . . As an engineer in that industry, you have tremendous opportunity to reduce that consumption and improve efficiency for the buildings you're working on.
>
> A lot of the buildings that were built in the 1980s and earlier had much less focus on energy use consumption. . . . If you can bring an old building up to speed, that's great, because [it will] save money and energy. With new systems, you can design systems to work in the most efficient way possible.

Source: "HVAC Engineer/Mechanical Engineer Interview." CAREERwise Education Green. MNSCU, 2016. Web. Accessed June 18, 2016.

What's the Big Idea?

Read the text carefully. Determine its main idea, and explain how the main idea is supported by details. Name at least two supporting details.

- Mechanical engineers design and build machines of all types.
- Mechanical engineering developed in different parts of the world. Leonardo da Vinci was one early mechanical engineer.
- Mechanical engineering is the largest and broadest branch of engineering. It contains several specialties. These include vehicle engineering, aerospace engineering, and manufacturing engineering.
- Mechanical engineers must take many math classes. They may also study science and robotics.
- Computers are critical tools in modern engineering.
- Mechanical engineers need to be curious and creative. They should like solving complex problems. They should work well with others.
- A bachelor's degree is required for most jobs. A graduate degree can lead to more job opportunities.
- The US military hires many mechanical engineers.

- Foreign language skills are useful for engineers who may work on projects in other countries.
- Mechanical engineers must keep safety in mind when designing their products.
- Today's mechanical engineers are making a difference in the fields of medicine and environmentally friendly technology, including alternative energy sources.

Tell the Tale

Chapter One of this book discusses some of the things that can be done with a 3D printer. Imagine you have a 3D printer to use for a week. What would you make? Write a 200-word essay about the items you would produce. What would you do with them?

Take a Stand

Chapter Three talks about the things mechanical engineers study. It suggests students should explore many interests. Sports, art, and music are mentioned. What activity do you think would most help a future engineer? Write an essay explaining your choice. How might the activity be useful in an engineering career?

Surprise Me

Chapter Two is about the history of mechanical engineering. After reading the book, what two or three facts about early mechanical engineering did you find most surprising? Write a few sentences about each fact. What surprised you most about them?

Dig Deeper

After reading this book, what questions do you still have about mechanical engineering? With an adult's help, find a few reliable sources that can help you answer your questions. Write a paragraph about what you learned.

GLOSSARY

acoustical
related to sound

aerospace
involving aircraft and space flight

clients
people or groups that use professional services

consultant
a person who works for different companies providing expert advice

doctorate
the highest degree awarded by a university

fossil fuels
fuel deposits from the earth, such as coal or gas

internship
a temporary job that provides training and may be paid or unpaid

pollute
to put harmful things into the air, water, or land

rover
a vehicle designed to explore the surfaces of places beyond Earth

thermal
relating to heat

LEARN MORE

Books

Koontz, Robin. *Robotics in the Real World.* Minneapolis, MN: Abdo Publishing, 2016.

Platt, Charles. *Make: Electronics: Learning by Discovery.* San Francisco, CA: Maker Media, 2015.

Snedden, Robert. *Mechanical Engineering and Simple Machines.* New York: Crabtree Publishing Company, 2013.

Websites

To learn more about STEM in the Real World, visit **booklinks.abdopublishing.com**. These links are routinely monitored and updated to provide the most current information available.

Visit **mycorelibrary.com** for free additional tools for teachers and students.

INDEX

Al-Jazari, 16
alternative energy, 38–39

careers, 13, 25–26, 28, 30–33, 41
cars, 5–6, 21, 23
Chang-Diaz, Franklin, 9
computers, 8, 9–10, 20, 23, 26
Curiosity rover, 8–9, 13

education, 21, 26–29
electricity, 20, 38
engineering branches, 8
engineering teams, 13, 27
environment, 38–39

graduate degrees, 28–29

Industrial Revolution, 18–20
internships, 28

Leonardo da Vinci, 16–18

machines, 7, 22
mathematics, 18, 26
medicine, 12, 30, 35–37
military, 9, 12, 31, 38

nanotechnology, 28, 36–37
NASA, 8, 9, 13
Newman, Ryan, 21
Nye, Bill, 30

safety, 27
salaries, 29
Sengupta, Anita, 13
spacecraft, 8–9, 13
steam power, 18–20

3D printers, 5–10, 20, 36

Zhang Heng, 15

ABOUT THE AUTHOR

M. M. Eboch writes fiction and nonfiction. Her novels include *The Genie's Gift*, a Middle Eastern fantasy; *The Eyes of Pharaoh*, a mystery in ancient Egypt; *The Well of Sacrifice*, a Mayan adventure; and the Haunted series.